BOOK ONE

Jazz Piano Basics

A Logical Method for Enhancing Your Jazzabilities

BY ERIC BAUMGARTNER

Jazz Piano Basics is a revised and vastly expanded version of *Jazzabilities*. This new method retains the unique approach of its predecessor while widening the scope to incorporate new concepts, exercises, and performance pieces designed as a comprehensive introduction to the fundamentals of jazz.

PLAYBACK+
Speed • Pitch • Balance • Loop

To access audio, visit:
www.halleonard.com/mylibrary
Enter Code
5494-8246-7536-4929

ISBN 978-1-4950-9495-8

WILLIS MUSIC

EXCLUSIVELY DISTRIBUTED BY

HAL • LEONARD®

7777 W. BLUEMOUND RD. P.O. BOX 13819 MILWAUKEE, WI 53213

Visit Hal Leonard Online at
www.halleonard.com

Preface

The study of jazz can be a daunting prospect, particularly for those coming from a classical music background. This is quite understandable since jazz music regularly involves tricky syncopated rhythms, complex harmonies, melodic phrases built from scales beyond major and minor—and improvisation! These are components not always covered in traditional study. It can be a challenge just knowing where to start. Many jazz books begin with a detailed look at theory—which *is* a vital part of any comprehensive study (including *this* series!)—but too much too soon can overwhelm and be intimidating. Without taking time to first build up a relevant musical vocabulary, theory runs the risk of remaining a purely intellectual exercise. This leads us to the unique approach of this series.

Jazz Piano Basics is a two-volume series that presents the fundamentals of jazz in a logical and accessible fashion, primarily through short, progressive exercises that can be grasped quickly in a teaching or self-taught situation. These exercises not only sharpen reading skills, but help build the strong rhythmic, melodic, and harmonic foundation necessary to better comprehend and apply the concepts of theory as they are presented. This series also takes a close look at improvisation, beginning with imitative melodic ear-training games, then expanding to include exploration of scales, harmonies, and chord voicings. In addition, there are performance pieces designed to reinforce the exercises, and comprehensive guidelines when new concepts or elements are introduced. Audio play-along tracks are included for every exercise, improvise section, and performance piece.

This series is ideal for anyone wishing to expand their "jazzabilities" and may be especially beneficial for those participating in a school jazz program. However, the practical benefits of this series are by no means limited to the budding young jazzer. The influence of jazz can be found in virtually every contemporary style of music—whether in the rich, complex chords of R&B, the syncopated swing rhythms of Broadway, or the improvised solos in rock and country music. Even if jazz is not your primary musical passion, having a fundamental knowledge of it is a practical and valuable asset.

It is my sincere hope that you enjoy this journey into jazz, and that this series may help you develop a deeper love and appreciation for this unique art form and for the many brilliant musicians who helped shape it.

Eric Baumgartner

Contents

Guide to the Exercises

With its bluesy melodies, colorful harmonies and infectious syncopated rhythms, jazz can be about as cool as it gets. This is readily apparent when *listening* to jazz music but may be less so when *reading* jazz music. The exercises within this series are brimming with all the cool characteristics of jazz. But in order to bring them to life, we need to be confident in our ability to accurately extract all the information from the page. In other words, we need sharp and dependable reading skills. So, before beginning the exercises, let's take a moment to fine-tune those reading skills, beginning with that all-important element, **RHYTHM**.

Rhythm isn't easy. It is arguably the trickiest aspect of music. To make matters worse, it often receives insufficient attention. Think about it: when faced with a new piece of music, there is great temptation to first focus on the notes, perhaps with only a passing thought (if any) to the rhythm. Each subsequent pass runs the risk of inadvertently reinforcing a wrong rhythm. This issue is compounded when turning to the world of jazz because the syncopated swing rhythms common in jazz (and in its stylistic brethren) tend to be more complex than those found in classical music of a comparable note-reading level. It is therefore no surprise that, in the study of jazz, one can quickly fall behind if insufficient attention is spent on rhythm. This is why we place **rhythm first**!

Each exercise begins with a short rhythmic pattern isolated above a musical excerpt:

The reason for this is simple: each rhythm must be mastered *before* the hands touch the keys. The most effective way to do this is to clap or tap the rhythm while **counting out loud**. Because eighth notes are present, it is necessary to divide the four beats by adding an "and" between each number (e.g., "1 and 2 and 3 and 4 and"). It is important to articulate *every* syllable of the counting regardless of the rhythm. The rhythmic pattern will vary exercise by exercise, but the steady pulse of the counting must remain consistent; otherwise, there is a risk of learning the rhythm incorrectly. It is remarkable how efficient and accurate one's approach to rhythm can become when counting out loud. This is not always the case when counting internally.

After you have mastered the rhythmic phrase, you are ready to play the exercise below it:

Note that the rhythmic pattern remains the same measure to measure. You won't see any tempo marks at the start of each exercise. This is not only to encourage you to work at your own pace but to also grant you license to explore different tempi to see how that may affect the feel of the exercise. Before playing, lock into the beat by counting out one full measure in preparation ("1 and 2 and 3 and 4 and"). Start as slowly as necessary to be confident of the notes and rhythms. Gradually increase the tempo, challenging yourself with faster and faster speeds while maintaining full control. It's best to work on one measure (or pattern) at a time, particularly as the exercises grow in complexity.

Audio Tracks. Once the patterns are in your fingers, you'll find these exercises great fun to play. But there's another cool aspect yet to explore: playing along with the audio tracks. This gives you the opportunity to join the band, playing your piano part alongside guitar, bass, drums, organ, and other instruments. Playing with the tracks is not only great fun but a terrific way to sharpen your rhythmic and performance skills.

Each exercise (and performance piece) will have two audio tracks. The first contains a recorded version of the exercise to a backing track and is labeled "Practice." The second contains only the backing track and is labeled "Performance." The Practice track is ideal to play along with while you are gaining confidence in the exercise but would still like the support of the recorded piano part. It will also be useful as an audio reference when faced with a new and particularly challenging rhythm. The Performance track is perfect for when you are ready to tackle the exercise without a safety net! Be sure to put in sufficient time to master the rhythm and prepare the exercise before attempting to play along with either track.

The Practice and Performance tracks for each exercise are set to the same tempo. As you first begin to work with a track you may find the tempo too brisk. Keep in mind that the *Playback+* function in MyLibrary (www.halleonard.com/MyLibrary) allows you to adjust the tempo for any track. This feature is common to other media players as well. Be sure to explore different tempi to find the optimal practice speed for each exercise. The *Playback+* function also allows you to set loop points for repetition of challenging (or fun!) measures.

Practice Tips. You'll spot useful tips throughout the book to guide you through new and/or challenging components. In general, be sure to take your time with all the material. Considering the short length of the exercises, it is fine to work on them in small manageable groupings, perhaps of two or three. Make sure, however, not to move on until you can perform each exercise, or group of exercises, accurately and confidently. To that end, playing along to the Performance audio track is the perfect way to evaluate both the accuracy and your level of confidence for any given exercise!

Guide to the *Improvise* Exercises

Each chapter features one or more improvisation exercises. Improvisation (or "improv" for short) is the art of creating or composing music spontaneously and is an essential element of jazz. However, the idea of creating music "on the spot" can be intimidating. Fear not! Improvisation, like any other musical discipline, is a skill that anyone can acquire with applied study and patience. We will begin our study not with complex scales and chord symbols, but with simple melodic and rhythmic imitation and variation. I find this a more accessible and engaging way to start, and it allows us to better focus on that important yet often elusive musical element, you guessed it: **RHYTHM**!

In each Improv exercise you will be provided a series of pitches to use for improvisation. For example:

You can trust these pitches to be "safe." That means that as you play along with the audio tracks or with the written-out accompaniment, regardless of the order you play them in, they *will* sound good. Melodically we start with just three pitches, so as not to steal focus from our primary goal of developing good rhythmic skills. We will eventually expand the melodic range to incorporate full scales.

Each Improv exercise includes a written-out accompaniment which will show the harmonic content of the audio tracks. It can be played by a teacher (or parent, sibling, etc.) in lieu of those tracks.

AUDIO TRACKS. The audio tracks vary throughout the book in style, key, and tempi and are designed to complement the exercises to which they are linked (there are directions at the bottom of each exercise page). There are two tracks available for each Improv exercise: "Question & Answer" (Q & A) and "Accompaniment."

Let's first experiment with improvising on the three notes in the example above:

1. Play the notes from low to high.
2. Play high to low.
3. Start with the middle note.
4. Try repeating some notes.
5. String together longer and longer sequences.
6. Vary these sequences every which way you can.

This can initially be a fun activity but you may find yourself quickly running out of ideas. This is not uncommon for beginning improvisers and can lead to a somewhat frustrating dead end.

So, let's try again. This time, think of a popular song such as "Happy Birthday." You may, as before, play the notes in any sequence, but this time lock into the slow, steady rhythm of "Happy Birthday." (Hint: SPEAK the words in rhythm as you play.) Now try again using the rhythm from one of your favorite pop songs, say, Bruno Mars's "Uptown Funk." Remember to only use the three pitches provided and to speak the words in rhythm as you play. Try another song you're very familiar with, maybe Neil Diamond's "Sweet Caroline" or Katy Perry's "Firework," or Queen's "We Will Rock You." Any song will do! Soon you will begin to find the results more pleasing and will gradually play with more authority and confidence. The difference is that you are playing these notes in tandem with a strong rhythmic phrase. Rhythm is the key. Improvising using familiar pop rhythms demonstrates this point but isn't a very practical tool in performance. Rather, we need to develop our own vocabulary of strong rhythmic phrases. This is where the Q & A track comes into play.

"Question & Answer" Track. Each Q & A track begins as a fun ear-training game. A recorded piano plays a short melodic phrase, often only one measure in length. Listen carefully to the phrase and then do your best to repeat it. The recorded piano will continue to challenge you with new phrases throughout the track. It won't take you long to get the hang of it!

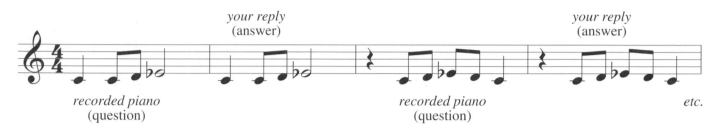

You should not only try to match the note sequence and rhythm of each phrase, but also do your best to match the feel by imitating dynamics and articulation. In other words, capture its attitude! Don't be distracted by a wrong or missed note: keep focused and always maintain a steady beat.

On subsequent playings, try answering each recorded phrase with your own variation. Start by slightly altering the rhythm or melody. Make sure your answer stays *related* to the question:

You needn't stop there! Challenge yourself to create new answers by varying the rhythms and melodies even further.

"Accompaniment" Track. The Question and Answer (Q & A) track will provide you the tools and the confidence to move on to the Accompaniment track. It is the same track as the Q & A but without the melodic piano "questions." These tracks offer the ideal accompaniment for free exploration. To ease into your explorations, however, it's best to start with firm footing. You will likely retain a few phrases from the Q & A track, so start with one of them. Keep your phrases short and separated by a few beats of rests. This will help keep your ideas concise and will give you time to mentally prepare the next phrase. You needn't feel limited to only the given pitches. Explore by adding a note or two above or below. If it sounds good, use it; if it sounds bad, don't! Trust your ear and never hesitate to experiment with additional or alternate pitches.

Also, think contrasts! Changing things up within or between phrases will help to keep ideas fresh and the listener's ear engaged. This can include contrasts in dynamics (e.g. soft vs loud), articulation (legato vs staccato), note lengths (short vs long), and register (octave up vs octave down). And remember, if you ever start to run out of steam, simply return to the Q & A track to recharge your creative battery.

PERFORMANCE PIECES. At the end of most chapters in this book is a performance piece to tie all the learned elements together. Practice them as you would a recital piece, with memorization as the goal. You may perform them as a solo or as part of the band with the aid of the audio tracks. Feel free to include a little improv as you progress and become more comfortable with the concept.

CHAPTER 1
Introductory Exercises

Let's begin by putting the guidelines on page 4 to the test with these simpler preparatory exercises. To reiterate, master the rhythm BEFORE playing each exercise, and be confident of each exercise before playing along with the audio tracks. Take your time in order to ensure accuracy and review the guidelines as needed. Such careful attention to detail will prepare you for the trickier exercises to come!

Clap or tap the rhythm of each exercise as you count out loud ("1 & 2 & 3 & 4 &"):

1.1

> Master each rhythm before you play.

1.2

> Reminder: there are two play-along tracks for every exercise: "Practice" includes the piano part and "Performance" is accompaniment only.

1.3

You are now ready to explore **Improv No. 1** on page 13.

The following exercises demonstrate the unique characteristics of meter in music. Even though all three rhythmic patterns contain two eighth notes followed by two quarter notes, they start at different points within the measure. Pay close attention to how the character of the phrase (Ex. 1.4) changes as it shifts to beat 2 (Ex. 1.5) and then to beat 3 (Ex. 1.6). This is because each beat within a measure (beats 1, 2, 3, and 4) has its own unique role—its own unique *feel*—which remains consistent measure to measure. *Where* a note is placed within the measure affects how we perceive it. This phenomenon will be easiest to hear and feel when playing along with the audio tracks.

1.4

Carefully observe the addition of articulation (staccatos, slurs, etc.)

1.5

1.6

You are now ready to explore **Improv No. 2** on page 13.

These next exercises are a bit more complex rhythmically. All three feature single eighth notes and eighth rests. As always, don't play the exercise until you are confident of the rhythm!

1.7

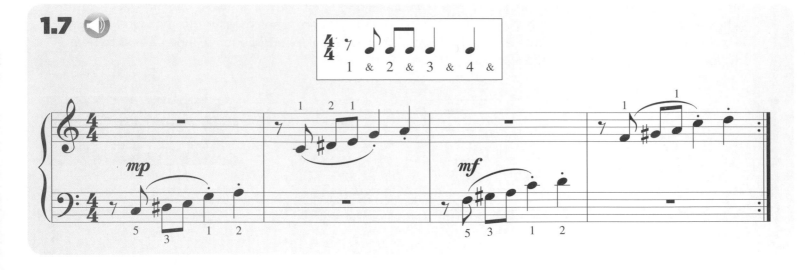

1.8

1.9

Hmm, this exercise doesn't appear to match the rhythm above. Ah, but if you look carefully you'll see that it does! The rhythmic pattern is merely divided between the hands and uses single (rather than beamed) eighth notes.

You are now ready to explore **Improv No. 3** on page 13.

Let's now add the dotted quarter note to the rhythmic phrases. It receives one-and-a-half beats—the same length as a quarter note tied to an eighth note.

1.10

This next rhythm is a bit tricky. After each single eighth note be sure to count a strong beat "1" so as not to lose the pulse.

1.11

1.12

You are now ready to explore **Improv No. 4** on page 14.

It is essential to lock into the feel and tempo of a piece *before* you play. This helps to guarantee a consistent and confident performance. It is for this reason that you hear preparatory beats at the start of each audio track. You can see this technique in action every time a drummer taps sticks together while counting in the band or when a conductor waves out a few beats with a baton before the orchestra plays or the choir sings. Slowly count out a measure in preparation ("1 & 2 & 3 & 4 &") before playing each new exercise.

1.13

1.14

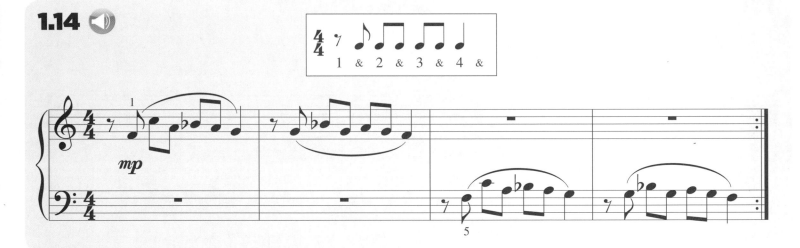

1.15

You are now ready to explore **Improv No. 5** on page 14.

Improvise

Begin every improv exercise with the Question & Answer audio track.

Improv No. 1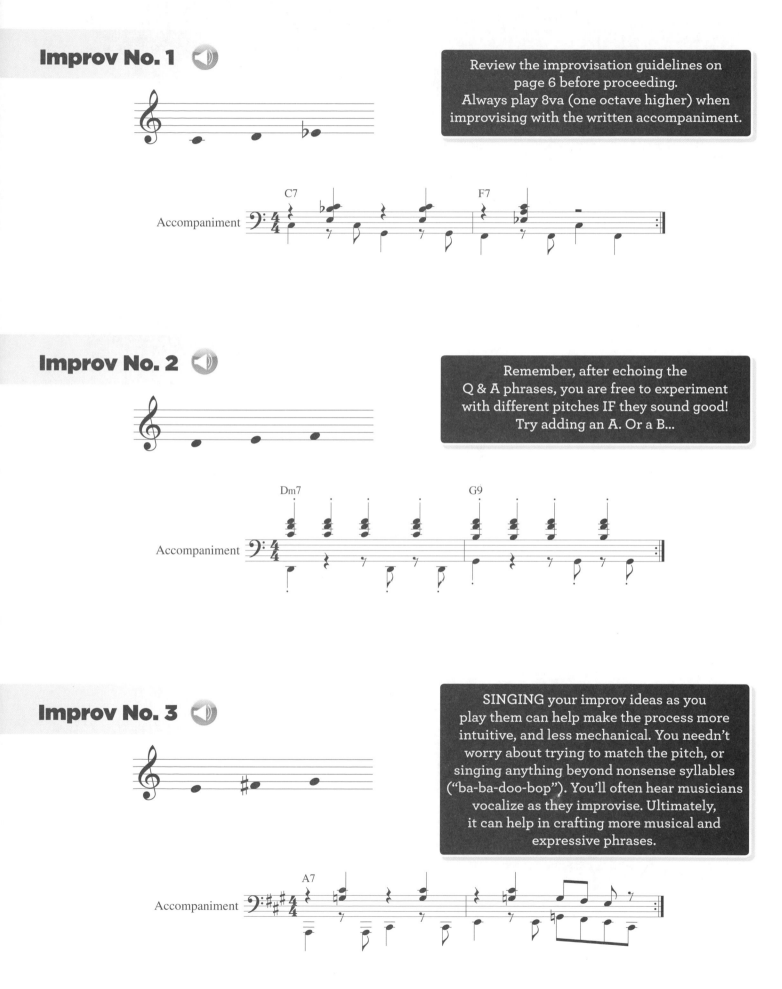

> Review the improvisation guidelines on page 6 before proceeding.
> Always play 8va (one octave higher) when improvising with the written accompaniment.

Improv No. 2

> Remember, after echoing the Q & A phrases, you are free to experiment with different pitches IF they sound good! Try adding an A. Or a B...

Improv No. 3

> SINGING your improv ideas as you play them can help make the process more intuitive, and less mechanical. You needn't worry about trying to match the pitch, or singing anything beyond nonsense syllables ("ba-ba-doo-bop"). You'll often hear musicians vocalize as they improvise. Ultimately, it can help in crafting more musical and expressive phrases.

Improv No. 4

Are you locking into the beat as you play? If so, you may find yourself bopping your head or tapping your foot without realizing it! No need to be self-conscious: you're in good company. Professional musicians do this all the time.

Accompaniment

Improv No. 5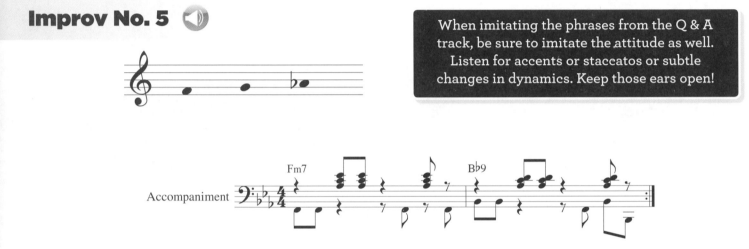

When imitating the phrases from the Q & A track, be sure to imitate the attitude as well. Listen for accents or staccatos or subtle changes in dynamics. Keep those ears open!

Accompaniment

PERFORMANCE PIECE. Here's a little rock 'n' roll to close out the chapter! Approach each phrase as you've done before: by first clapping or tapping the rhythm. Work measure by measure, slowly piecing it all together as you gain control. Never be shy about penciling in your own counting for a tricky spot; it's simplest to use a plus sign for the "ands" (e.g., **1 + 2 + 3 + 4 +**).

Funkasaurus

Eric Baumgartner

Moving steadily (with attitude!)

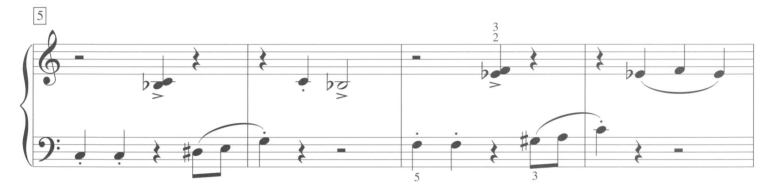

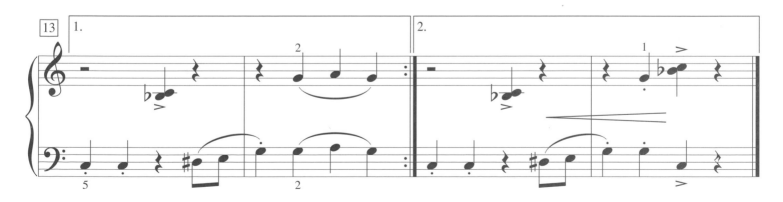

CHAPTER 2
Swing It!

Swing is one of the defining (and most delightfully infectious!) characteristics of jazz. It is the practice of playing the eighth notes unevenly—the first of each pair being long, the second short. Swing is very closely associated with jazz music but is by no means *limited* to jazz music. You find examples of swing in every contemporary style (blues, rock, hip hop, country, R&B, Broadway, etc.), sometimes alternately labeled as "shuffle," "boogie," or to be played "with a lilt."

Swung eighth notes are played in long-short pairs. But how long is long? How short is short? A general rule is that the first note be twice the length of the second. Musicians are free, however, to vary these lengths slightly for purposes of contrast and expression. We'll explore this aspect in upcoming Improv exercises.

If a piece of music is meant to be swung, you will find an instruction to do so next to the tempo marking. Remember that an alternate term is often used (see above) or it may instruct you with this symbol:

This indicates that the eighth notes should be played as a triplet figure: the first lasting 2/3 of the beat, the second 1/3. (More about triplets in Chapter 7.)

You may now and then see alternate methods to notate swing, other than by using eighth notes. The most common is the dotted eighth and sixteenth note pairing: ♪. However, this notation is far from ideal. For one thing, if played literally it is far too "strict" sounding. It can also be quite a challenge to read, particularly when combined with ties and rests. Fortunately, this variant is seldom used anymore as jazz pedagogy becomes more and more standardized. You can now count on eighth notes being used to notate swing rhythms in almost every modern music publication as well as in school jazz programs, universities, and in professional circles.

Here's a nifty little preparatory exercise (Ex. 2.1). It clearly demonstrates the difference in feel between swung and straight eighth notes. The audio track will play through the exercise four times: the 1st and 3rd using swing eighth notes, the 2nd and 4th using straight eighths. With the support of the audio track, you will have no trouble at all feeling the shift and locking into the groove!

2.1 🔊

To ensure a proper swing feel, it's important to lock into the swing pulse *before* clapping or tapping the rhythm. Start by counting out a few preparatory measures until you can "speak" the swing. The numbers are the long eighth notes, the "ands" are the short ones:

one   and   two   and   three   and   four   and

(long   short   long   short   long   short   long   short)

Retain the swing feel as you clap or tap these new rhythms and as you play the following exercises:

2.2

2.3

2.4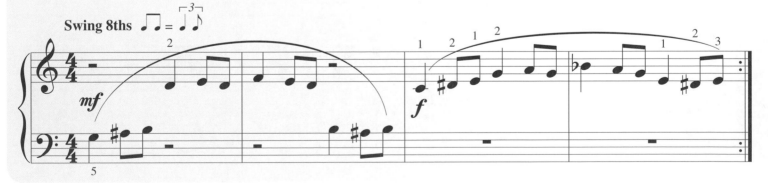

You are now ready to explore **Improv No. 6** on page 22.

Be mindful of rests. *Always* give them the same rhythmic respect you'd give a note.

2.5

2.6

2.7

You are now ready to explore **Improv No. 7** on page 22.

Another appealing characteristic of jazz is *syncopation*. This is when the weak pulse (the "and") is emphasized. This rhythmic device is not limited to the world of jazz—far from it. Once you start looking you'll find examples of it absolutely everywhere in music, including in Beethoven, Chopin, and Bach!

Syncopated rhythms can be tricky to feel and a challenge to read since they frequently involve ties. Let's focus on just one example. Each exercise on this page syncopates the "and" of beat 2. As you tie the note, be sure to feel a strong beat "3" and maintain that steady pulse.

2.8

2.9

2.10

You are now ready to explore **Improv No. 8** on page 22.

We now know quite well that swung eighth notes are played in long-short pairs. That's easy enough when a phrase starts on the long eighth, but what about when it starts on the short one? That little change has tripped up many a jazz novice! But, as long as you are properly locked into the swing pulse and counting correctly, it should be an easy adjustment. Let's now put you to the challenge. The following rhythmic phrases all start with a short eighth.

2.11

2.12

2.13

You are now ready to explore **Improv No. 9** on page 23.

As the exercises grow in complexity, it's a good idea to master the hands separately before combining them.

2.14

2.15

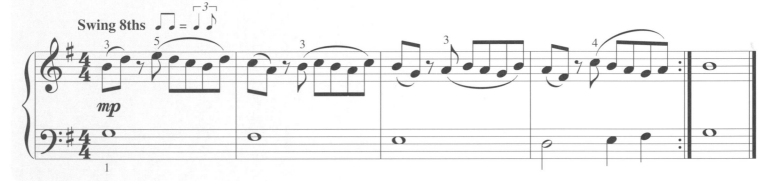

2.16

You are now ready to explore **Improv No. 10** on page 23.

Improvise

Our improvisation exercises will also switch to swing. Don't worry, the switch will be a breeze! As always, start by imitating the recorded piano questions on the Q & A track. The swing pulse is prominent and you should find it easy to follow.

Improv No. 6

Improv No. 7

Improv No. 8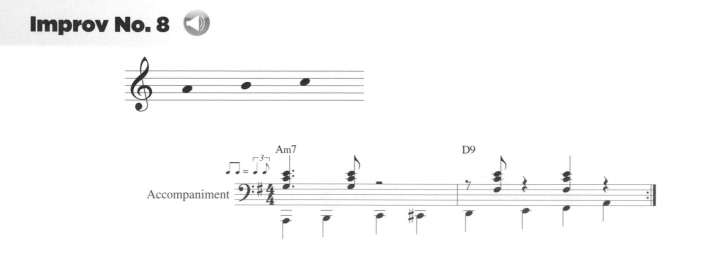

Improv No. 9

Have you noticed that the Q & A tracks often use rhythmic phrases taken from the exercises? Listen carefully and you'll hear the rhythms of the three associated exercises from page 20 used in this Q & A track. Extra credit if you can visualize how that notated rhythmic pattern would look as you play it!

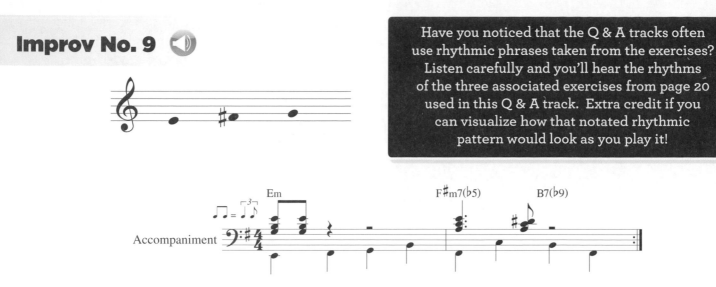

Improv No. 10

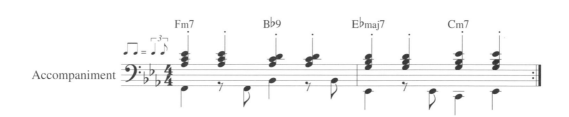

PERFORMANCE PIECE. "Midtown Strut" is the perfect capper to our opening swing section! Like "Funkasaurus," it contains only a handful of unique rhythmic phrases, despite its longer length. The middle part employs a "walking" left-hand bass, a common (and really cool) feature of jazz. (We'll return to the walking bass in more detail for Book 2.)

Midtown Strut

Eric Baumgartner

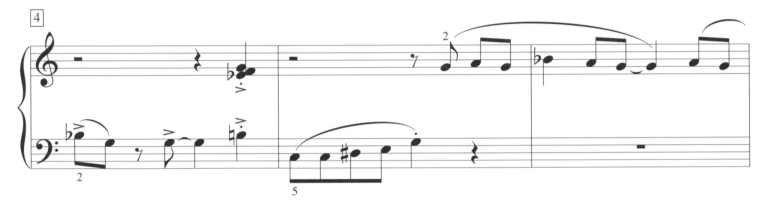

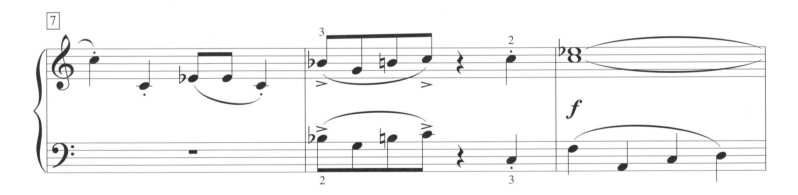

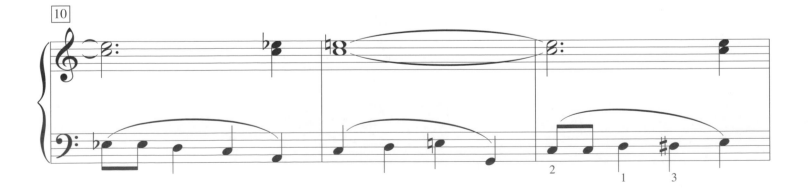

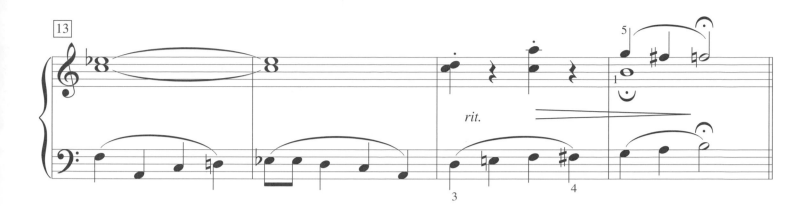

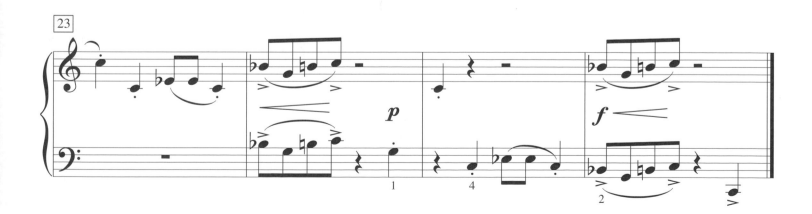

CHAPTER 3
Pickup Notes

A pickup, or *anacrusis*, is a note (or series of notes) that precedes the first full measure of a piece:

Pickup notes

It would appear these pickup notes are part of a very short measure, but pickup notes are simply the tail end of a partial measure. Here is how that same phrase looks when the whole measure is presented:

Pickup notes

Adding the rests makes it easy to see that the phrase begins on beat 4, and that is how you should approach pickup notes: by mentally adding in the rests and counting from the beginning of the partial measure.

All the exercises in this chapter begin with pickup measures of varying length. However, the rhythmic exercises in the next several pages will include rests at the start of each phrase so that you can easily count from the beginning of the measure. To illustrate, here is a rhythmic figure with a pickup measure of three eighth notes:

And here it is with the rests and counting included:

The pickup measures will be presented in their standard fashion for the music exercises. It will be your job to mentally add in the rests and count in your preparatory beats from the beginning of the measure.

In Ex. 3.1, notice the final measure is also a partial measure. Its length is altered so that when repeating back to the beginning the two partials add up to one complete measure. (You may have already come across this notation in classical pieces you've studied.) In this case, the final measure contains beats 1 and 2; the pickup measure, beats 3 and 4. This makes for a seamless repeat, as demonstrated nicely in the audio track.

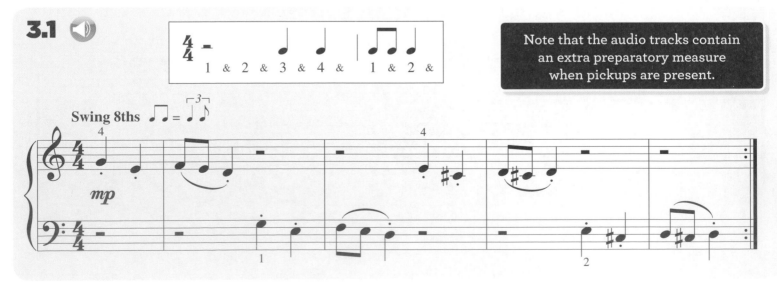

Note that the audio tracks contain an extra preparatory measure when pickups are present.

You'll see the professionals approach pickup notes this same way: counting from the beginning of the partial measure. Let's return to our rock band example from page 12, this time with pickups. The drummer begins counting in from beat 1 as usual, but this time the band enters *before* the next measure to accommodate the pickups. Experienced musicians will instinctively feel the proper placement of pickup notes.

3.2

3.3

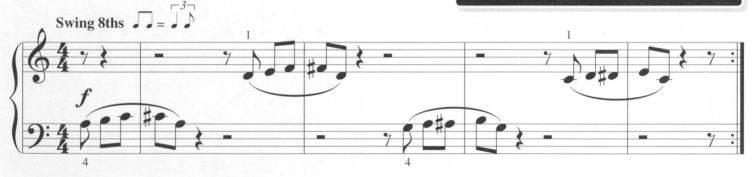

Pickup measure = 1-1/2 beats, final measure = 2-1/2 beats. The math is a little trickier but the results are the same, adding up to 4 beats and one complete measure.

3.4

You are now ready to explore **Improv No. 11** on page 30.

3.5

3.6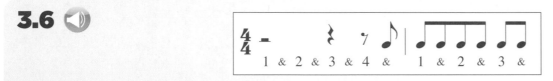

3.7

You are now ready to explore **Improv No. 12** on page 31.

The starting rests will now be removed from the rhythmic pickup measures. Continue to count from beat 1 for all pickup measures, just as if the rests were still present!

3.8

3.9

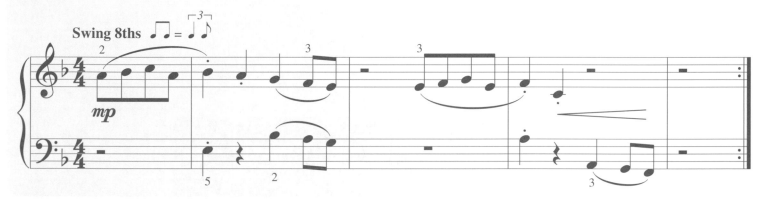

3.10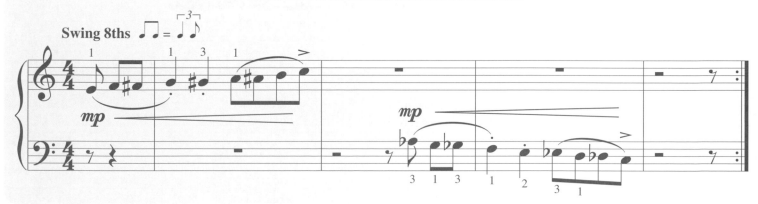

You are now ready to explore **Improv No. 13** on page 31.

Improvise

A fourth note is now added to the Improvise exercises. The Q & A track will reflect this by presenting up to four different possible pitches for each question. Fingering is offered as a suggestion. You're welcome to experiment with other combinations. And, when not imitating the Q & A questions, experiment with adding or altering pitches. Search for those notes that sound best with the accompaniment.

Improv No. 11

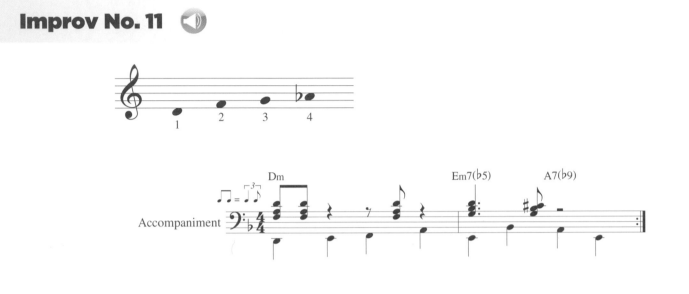

You may have noticed subtle variations in the length of swung eighth notes on the Q & A tracks. The long-short pairs might be played a bit more evenly or rather "lazily" (slightly late, just after the beat). These rhythmic variations can provide added expression, personality, and even humor to your ideas and may help prevent rhythms from sounding too mechanical. Keep listening closely to the questions and do your best to imitate the notes as well as their nuances.

Improv No. 12

Improv No. 13

Performance Piece. We close out this section with another swingin' number! The short opening phrase provides the melodic spark for the entire first section. Look for its repetition, variation, and expansion; and as always, be confident of each right-hand phrase before adding the left.

Jumpin' Jazz

Eric Baumgartner

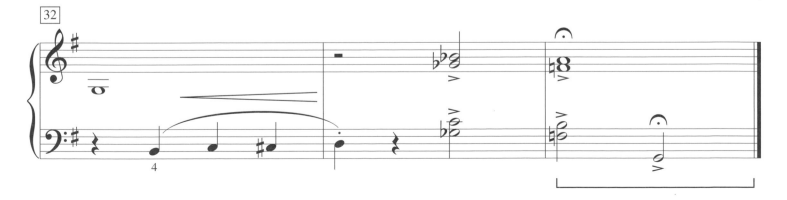

CHAPTER 4
Latin Jazz

The term "Latin jazz" refers to jazz music that contains Latin American rhythms. These rhythms are often highly syncopated but, unlike other jazz styles, are typically performed using straight, rather than swung, eighth notes. Popular examples of Latin jazz include the bossa nova, samba, and Afro-Cuban music. The following exercises are modeled after these popular Latin jazz styles.

4.1

4.2

4.3

You are now ready to explore **Improv No. 14** on page 36.

4.4 🔊

For a bit of fun, let's break away from Latin jazz for the moment to present two styles that also feature syncopation and straight (even) eighth notes. First: Caribbean.

4.5 🔊

Next, West Coast surf!

4.6 🔊

You are now ready to explore **Improv No. 15** on page 36.

Improvise

Improv No. 14

Improv No. 15

PERFORMANCE PIECE. "Stepping Out" is composed in a Latin jazz style and sports a few tricky sequences, such as when each hand is playing a different syncopated rhythm (e.g. measures 6 through 8). Write in the counts for any tricky measure (**1 + 2 + 3 + 4 +**). This will help you visually align the two parts for more efficient and accurate practicing. The backing track for this piece is brisk, so be prepared!

Stepping Out

Eric Baumgartner

CHAPTER 5
Jazz Waltz

Like its traditional European cousin, the jazz waltz is played in 3/4 time, but in a syncopated and swung style. The jazz waltz remains very popular amongst jazz artists due in no small part to the change of meter. This shift provides a welcome contrast to the dominant 4/4 time signature.

Some of the best-loved jazz waltz pieces were sourced from outside the world of jazz, such as musicals ("My Favorite Things" from *The Sound of Music*) and animated films ("Someday My Prince Will Come" and "Alice in Wonderland"). However, there are also many jazz waltz standards written by jazz artists. You might recognize Toots Thielemans's "Bluesette" and Bill Evans's "Waltz for Debby."

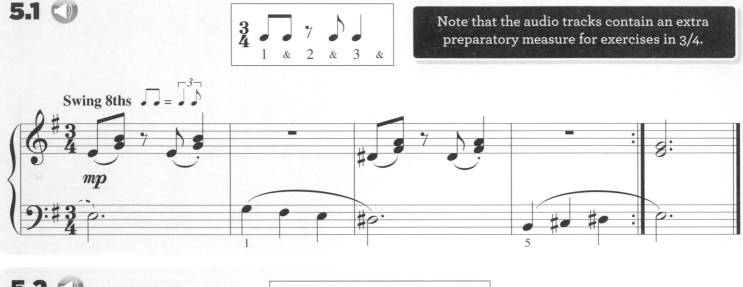

Note that the audio tracks contain an extra preparatory measure for exercises in 3/4.

You are now ready to explore **Improv No. 16** on page 40.

5.4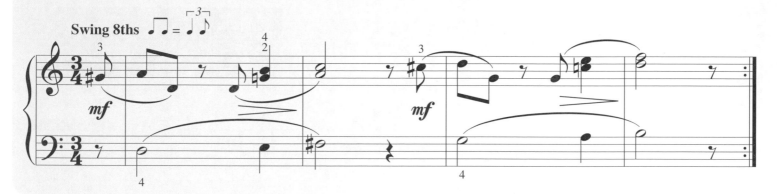

5.5

5.6

You are now ready to explore **Improv No. 17** on page 40.

Improvise

Improv No. 16

> To ease you into the change of meter, this exercise will use only three melodic pitches.

Improv No. 17

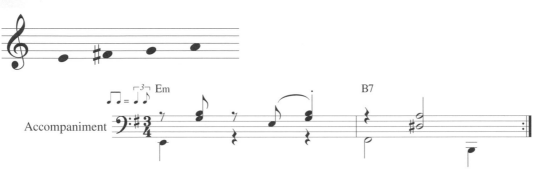

Performance Piece. "Petite Waltz" is an elegant and subtle piece requiring confident control and a light touch (note that the dynamics rarely rise above *mezzo piano*). The second 8-measure phrase (measures 9 to 16) may be a challenge. The flowing right-hand melody is accompanied by a syncopated left-hand counter line. But, note the rhythmic repetition! Once you have measures 9 and 10 in your fingers, the remaining measures should come together quickly.

Petite Waltz

Eric Baumgartner

Swift and nimble

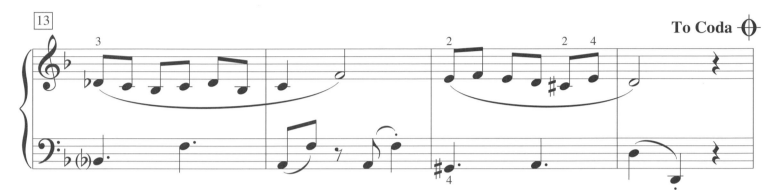

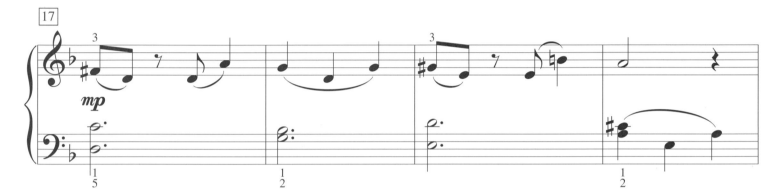

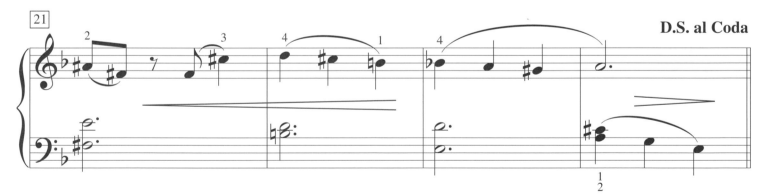

D.S. al Coda

two grace notes (see page 44)

CHAPTER 6
Classic & Cool

The exercises in this chapter are inspired by various standards from the classic jazz era of the 1940s and 50s. Remain consistent and patient in your approach as you'll now be challenged with longer phrases, tricky melodic bits, and some active left hand "comping" (an abbreviated term jazz musicians use to mean "accompanying").

You are now ready to explore **Improv No. 18** on page 47.

The next four exercises pay homage to the music of **Thelonious Monk** (1917-1982). His compositions were known for their quirky rhythmic shifts, bluesy harmonies, and chromaticism.

6.4

6.5

6.6

You are now ready to explore **Improv No. 19** on page 47.

GRACE NOTES. The grace note is a short ornamental note commonly used to add a bluesy touch to a phrase. It is exceedingly popular in all types of contemporary music. Even though it looks like a tiny eighth note, it does not add time to a measure. Rather, it is coupled with a longer standard note:

When a grace note is present it is a good idea to first play the phrase without it, because its presence could distract you from learning the phrase accurately. Since the grace note adds no time to the measure, the counting remains the same with or without it:

Once you have successfully learned the phrase, adding the grace note is easy.

There is no exact science for playing a grace note in jazz. It can be played at the same time as the standard note or just prior. The trick is to release it immediately so it doesn't detract from the sound of the more important standard note.

Listen closely to the audio tracks for the upcoming exercises (as well as for Improv No. 20) to hear examples of how grace notes are commonly played.

6.8

6.9

6.10

You are now ready to explore **Improv No. 20** on page 47.

These exercises are modeled after the sophisticated stylings of **Duke Ellington** (1899-1974). He was a prominent composer and pianist best remembered as the leader of various big bands that bore his name from the 1920s up until the 1970s.

6.11

6.12

6.13

You are now ready to explore **Improv No. 21** on page 47.

Improvise

Improv No. 18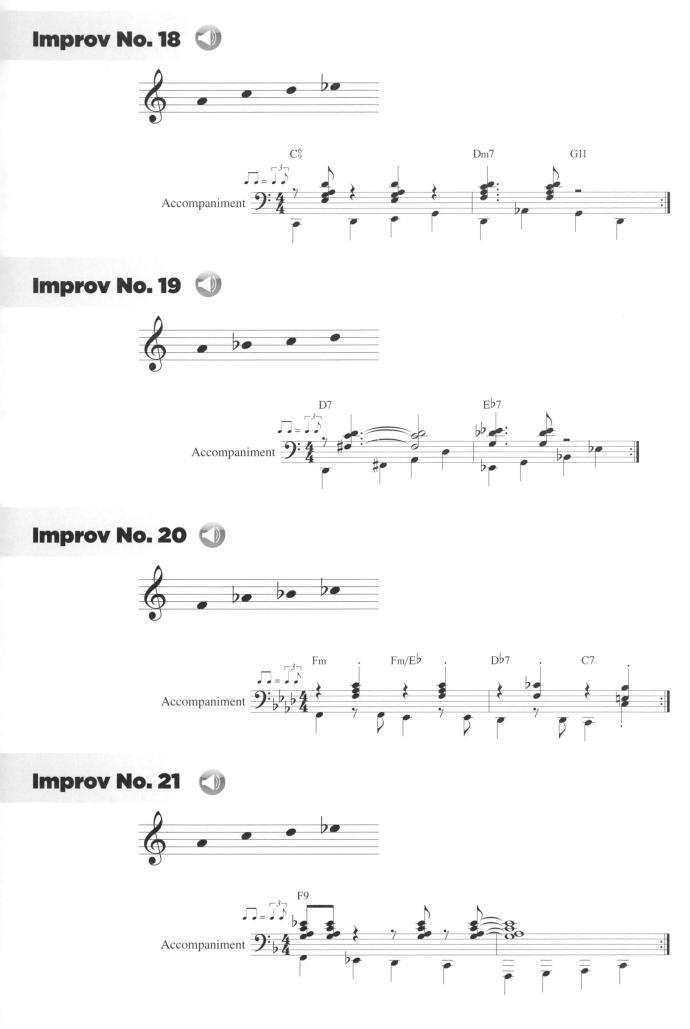

Improv No. 19

Improv No. 20

Improv No. 21

Elling Tones

Eric Baumgartner

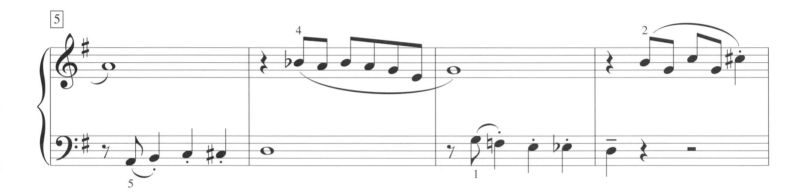

CHAPTER 7
Triplets

It's remarkable how much mileage you can get with eighth notes. Up to this point we've seen only a small sample of the rhythmic possibilities of eighth notes when combined with rests and notes of longer durations. In fact, so great are these possibilities that jazz musicians frequently find no need to stretch beyond the eighth note when composing melodies, and this is why we've focused so diligently thus far on the mighty eighth note. However, there is another rhythmic figure common in jazz that deserves our attention and respect: the **triplet**. You've seen it as part of the rhythmic indicator that has prefaced many of the exercises thus far.

A triplet is a group of three notes played in a space of two. For example, an eighth-note triplet equals the length of two eighth notes, and a quarter-note triplet equals the length of two quarter notes:

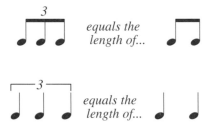

Eighth-note triplets are by far the most common type and can simply be referred to as "triplets."

You may already be familiar with triplets but perhaps not in the context of swing. The swing pulse uniquely unites triplets and eighth notes, making them more closely related than when used in a traditional straight pulse. This is because the long-short pulse of swing is essentially a triplet pulse with the first two notes tied:

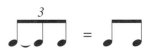

Once locked into the swing pulse, it becomes easy to feel or to play the triplet. Let's practice. The exercise below alternates between a measure of triplets and a measure of swung eighth notes. Clap or tap the rhythm as you say the word "trip-a-let" over and over. The long-short pairs of the eighth notes will land only on the "trip" and "let":

trip - a - let, trip - a - let, trip - a - let, trip - a - let, trip - a - let, trip - a - let, trip - a - let, trip - a - let

Keep at it until you can easily switch between the two measures without interrupting the steady "trip-a-let, trip-a-let" counting.

It would be useful, at this point, to adjust our counting for triplets. I suggest using "one and uh, two and uh," etc. (expressed in the exercises as "1 & a, 2 & a"). As long as you're faithfully locking into the long-short swing pulse, you can stick to "one and two and," etc. for everything else. Take some time to clap/tap and count this exercise before moving on:

You'll no longer see the reminder to "Swing 8ths" over the musical excerpt; just this universal symbol, which you should already be familiar with:

7.1 🔊

* Don't mistake the triplet mark for a fingering! The triplet '3' is usually larger and *italicized*.

7.2

7.3

7.4

You are now ready to explore **Improv No. 22** on page 57.

7.5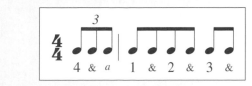

7.6

7.7

You are now ready to explore **Improv No. 23** on page 57.

Take note of the shift back to the jazz waltz meter for all the exercises on this page.

7.8 🔊

7.9 🔊

7.10 🔊

You are now ready to explore **Improv No. 24** on page 57.

The next few exercises are to be played with straight, not swung, eighth notes. This may present a challenge. It is trickier to feel a triplet when it's framed by straight eighth notes. Listen to the audio track for reference.

7.11

7.12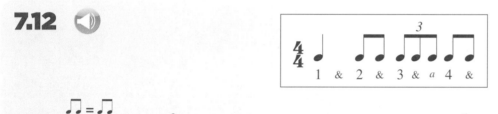
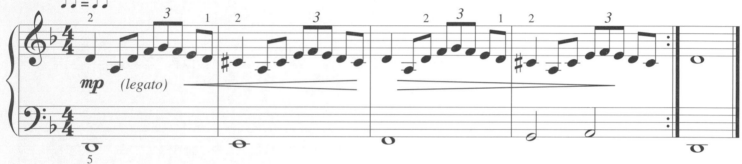

7.13

You are now ready to explore **Improv No. 25** on page 57.

Most of the triplets on this page have a new look: the first note has been replaced by a rest. This is a common—if somewhat strange-looking—rhythmic variation. Feel and count the rest just as you would if it were a note.

7.14

7.15

7.16

You are now ready to explore **Improv No. 26** on page 58.

Improvise

Improv No. 22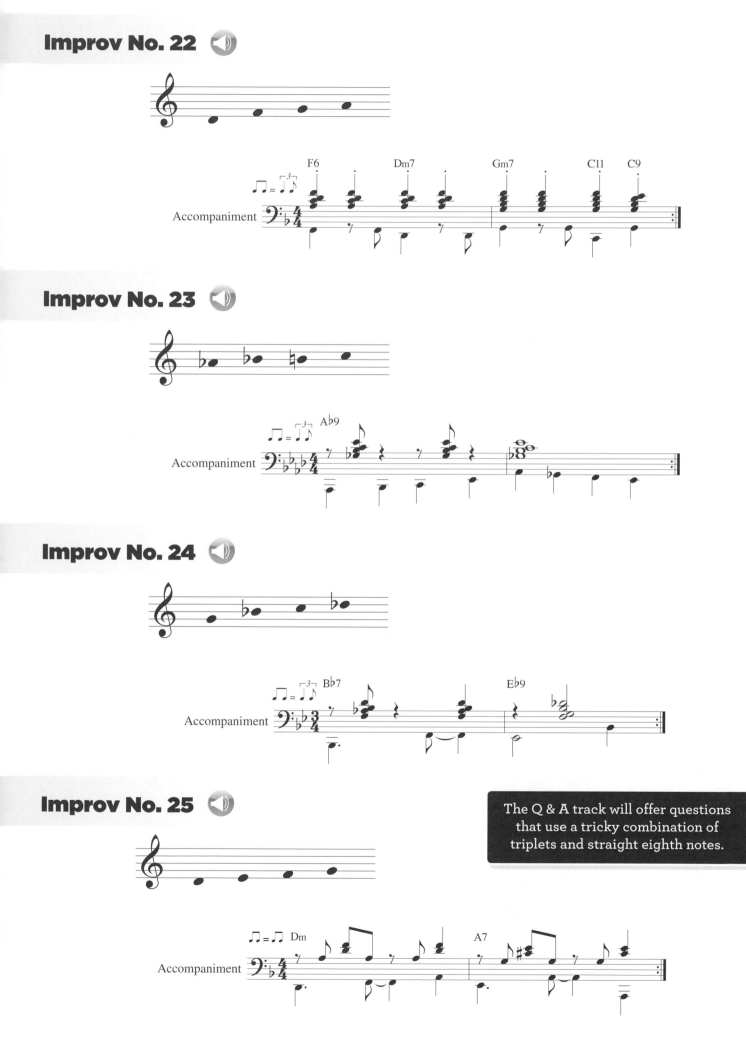

Improv No. 23

Improv No. 24

Improv No. 25

The Q & A track will offer questions that use a tricky combination of triplets and straight eighth notes.

Performance Piece. The rhythmic phrases in "Blue Bop" are not as complex as those of the preceding exercises, and the phrases tend to repeat over and over. However, what it lacks in rhythmic complexity it makes up for in the challenging hand movements: each hand has plenty of quick leaps! Focus first on the hands individually—phrase by phrase—before combining them.

Blue Bop

Eric Baumgartner

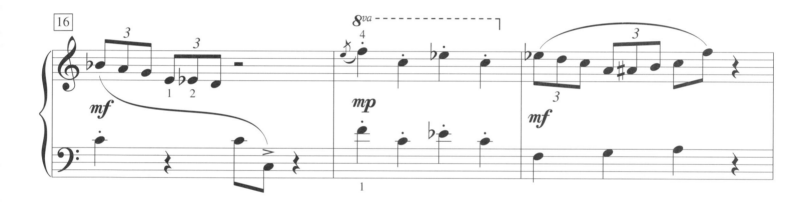

CHAPTER 8
The (Major) Pentatonic Scale

This chapter signals an exciting new phase in our exploration of jazz as we begin a more detailed look into the world of melody and harmony. We start with a scale that, once learned, provides great insight into the construction of countless melodies and improvised solos.

The pentatonic scale is surely the most universal (and universally applicable!) scale in all of music. It dates back thousands of years and can be found all over the world. It consists of five pitches and is a close relative of the major scale:

Compare the two scales. They are quite similar, the difference being two fewer pitches for the pentatonic. You can construct a pentatonic scale quite quickly by simply omitting the 4th and 7th tones from any major scale (in this example: F and B).

You may also refer to this scale as the *major* pentatonic. This is useful when distinguishing it from the minor pentatonic scale (profiled in the next chapter). However, "pentatonic" will suffice for our purposes throughout the rest of this chapter, as it does in most colloquial musical circles.

The pentatonic scale is a great place to start when trying to better understand the melodic content used in composition and improvisation. It is enormously popular and can be found in virtually every musical style. Examples in jazz include the opening melodic phrases from both George Gershwin's "Someone to Watch Over Me" and Duke Ellington's "In a Sentimental Mood." Pop examples include the opening guitar riff in "My Girl" by the Temptations as well as the vocal melodies of "Shake It Off" by Taylor Swift, "Beautiful Boy" by John Lennon, and "Roar" by Katy Perry.

Take a moment to get to know the notes. Move up and down the scale and then connect to neighboring octaves. Explore changing direction and repeating notes. At this point, moving stepwise (rather than skipping or leaping scale tones) will give you the most pleasing results. You might have already happened upon a few familiar riffs or melodies. Not surprising: the pentatonic scale can be found *everywhere*!

We'll be using several pentatonic scales in the upcoming exercises. For each new scale, it will be helpful to review its construction and compare it to the major. Let's do that now for the F Major and F (major) pentatonic scales:

Chord Symbols. Another new component to the exercises in this chapter is the chord symbol. Chord symbols are very useful for musicians. They provide a quick and easy summary of the harmony used at any particular point in a piece. You have no doubt already spotted their use in the accompaniments within the Improvise sections. An experienced musician may refer to nothing more than a series of chord symbols when performing, creating from them an appropriate arrangement from scratch.

Similarly, a *lead sheet* is a single staff of music containing notes that outline a melody along with chord symbols. A collection of lead sheets is often referred to as a *fake book*—meaning the player must "fake" (create) their own arrangement. (Lead sheets will be explored in Book 2 of this series.)

Chord symbols will be your window into the harmonic content for all upcoming exercises (and as heard on the audio tracks). You will find three different chord types—major, minor, and dominant—represented throughout the rest of Book 1:

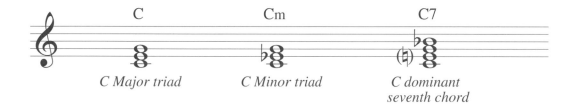

C Major triad   C Minor triad   C dominant
                                    seventh chord

You may be less familiar with the third chord type: the *dominant seventh*. You won't see this chord in the chord symbols until the final chapter. We will hold off a detailed study on the construction of the dominant seventh until Book 2. Do your best to get to know the shape and sound of the chord when it appears in Chapter 11.

As you practice, always be observant of the chord symbol above to see how the melodic content connects to it. It will soon become apparent that each pentatonic scale blends beautifully with the major chord of the same root (for example, C pentatonic scale with C Major chord). For extra credit, at any point as you're learning a new melodic phrase, you may play a chord with the other hand as a way to more fully hear and explore the relationship between melody and harmony.

This page features two pentatonic scales: C and F. Each phrase is first introduced in C, then shifts to F.

8.1

8.2

8.3

You are now ready to explore **Improv No. 27** on page 65.

This page features the D and G pentatonic scales. How quickly can you form those scales using the guidelines from page 60?

8.4

8.5

8.6

You are now ready to explore **Improv No. 28** on page 65.

We'll take a brief look now at some flat-key pentatonic scales, starting with B-flat. Note that this exercise contains a new rhythmic variation: the last triplet note is tied.

8.8

Notice that the left hand in the following exercise is simply a descending E-flat scale.

The black keys on the piano provide a quick and easy way in which to form the pentatonic scale. Start on a G-flat and work your way up (or down) on black keys to the next G-flat: an instant pentatonic scale! Here's a G-flat pentatonic exercise:

You are now ready to explore **Improvs No. 29** and **30** on page 66.

Improvise

Our source notes for this session will be the C pentatonic scale. The extra available pitches will present new possibilities and new challenges. As always, it's best to begin by imitating the questions on the Q & A track. They will start on (or near) Middle C and use only the neighboring pentatonic tones above or below (we are not confined to one octave). After several phrases, the questions will move a little higher but will still not have a large melodic range. This is to prevent the ear training game from becoming too complex, and it is also to illustrate that one does not need to use a large number of different pitches to construct effective phrases.

Keep this in mind as you play with the Accompaniment track. Focus on developing solid phrases for a small part of the scale before widening your scope. Remember that you don't have to limit yourself to play within one octave. Some very effective melodic lines can be found by incorporating notes both above and below any C.

Improv No. 27

As you play along to the audio track of this next improv, you may notice the chords shifting. In fact, there are four different chords used in the accompaniment. Yet, we only need one scale in our improvisation! When the chords of a piece are constructed from the same key (in this case, G), it is often desirable to stick to a single scale when improvising. This not only makes soloing more manageable but often more musical, lending a sense of cohesion and continuity to the phrases. An example is the guitar solo from the Beatles song "Let It Be." The chord harmonies shift every two beats, yet George Harrison plays only notes from the C pentatonic scale throughout.

Improv No. 28

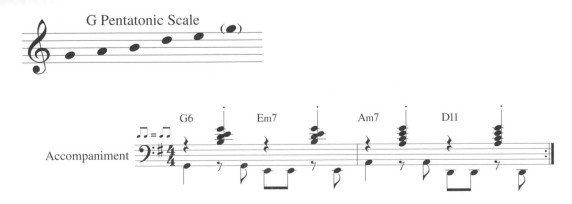

Unlike jazz artists, rock and pop artists often use chord progressions built from one single key. (There are many notable exceptions, including groups like Steely Dan and Yes.) Since the pentatonic scale is so effective for improvising in this situation, it's no surprise that we can find seemingly endless examples of pentatonic solos within the world of rock and pop. And since guitar is often the instrument of choice for those styles, you may look to any number of prominent guitarists for examples. For starters, check out the solos of such classic rock artists as Jimmy Page (Led Zeppelin), Eric Clapton (solo or with Cream), or Jimi Hendrix. As your ear becomes more and more attuned to the sound of the pentatonic scale, you will begin to identify it more easily and spot its use more frequently. It is a very popular scale!

Improv No. 29

Improv No. 30

CHAPTER 9
The Minor Pentatonic Scale

This new scale will be a breeze to learn. All it takes is a brief introduction to the concept of relative major and minor, which you may already know something about! For every major scale, there is a minor scale that shares the same notes and the same key signature. For example, the C Major scale shares the same notes with the A natural minor scale. Their shared key signature contains no sharps or flats:

Major and minor scales that have this connection are said to be relative: C is the relative major of A Minor, A is the relative minor of C Major. Take a moment to explore some other relative major/minor pairings. Here are some ways to quickly make the connection:

Major: from the root, jump to the 6th scale tone or count down three half steps to determine the minor.

Minor: from the root, jump to the 3rd scale tone or count up three half steps.

This special major/minor relationship provides the knowledgeable musician with a wealth of useful applications. So much so that each pairing eventually becomes second nature, e.g. C Major/A Minor, G Major/E Minor, D Major/B Minor, etc.

The good news is that this relative major/minor pairing is identical for pentatonic scales! That is, every major pentatonic scale has a relative minor pentatonic scale that shares the same notes. (For clarity I'm using the more formal "*major* pentatonic" rather than just "pentatonic." Review previous chapter as needed.) Just as C Major and A Minor are relative, C Major *pentatonic* and A Minor *pentatonic* are relative as well:

So, if the scales consist of the same notes, why bother calling them by different names? The answer is: **context**. In C Major, the note "C" is the anchor; the tonal center. Melodic phrases often work best when not straying too far away from it. Phrases certainly sound more complete when ending with it. In A Minor, the tonal center shifts to A and melodic phrases often shift to reflect it. The way we perceive a note or notes depends on the key or chord it's coupled with. To illustrate, play an A Minor chord with your left hand, near middle C (A-C-E). Now, with your right hand, add the note A above it. Move your left hand up a bit now to play a C Major chord (C-E-G). Now add that same A with your right. Notice how the flavor of that right hand A has completely changed? **Understanding the harmonic context leads to better melodic choices, which leads to better improvisation.**

The minor pentatonic scale is a favorite for rock and heavy metal artists. You'll hear its use prominently in the opening guitar riffs of Led Zeppelin's "Heartbreaker," Jimi Hendrix's "Purple Haze," and Kansas's "Carry On Wayward Son." A pop example would be the vocal melody of Adele's "Hello"; a jazz example is George Gershwin's "Summertime" (all but one note).

Keep the relative major/minor relationships in mind as you play the following minor pentatonic exercises. Compare the A Minor and D Minor patterns below to the C and F patterns from the previous chapter (page 62).

RELATIVE KEYS
C Major – A Minor
F Major – D Minor

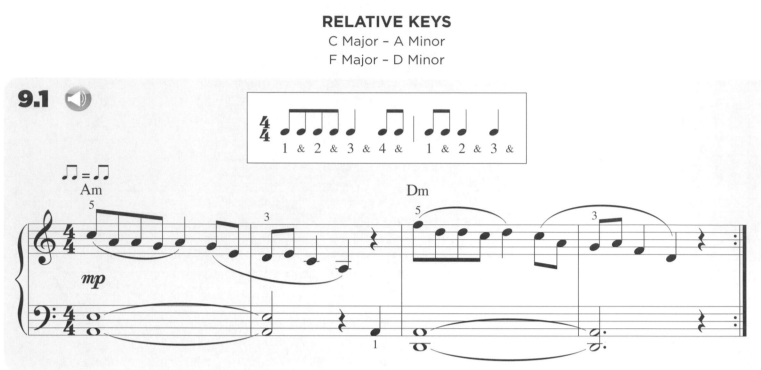

Compare the B Minor and E Minor patterns below to the D and G patterns from page 63.

RELATIVE KEYS
D Major – B Minor
G Major – E Minor

B-flat Major and G Minor are relative keys. This exercise illustrates how the same melodic phrase may be used for both chords. Notice how the feel of the phrase subtly changes with the shift of harmony.

9.3

E-flat Major and C Minor form another pair of relative keys. This exercise is similar to the one above, demonstrating how a single set of pentatonic scale tones can be used for a relative pairing.

9.4

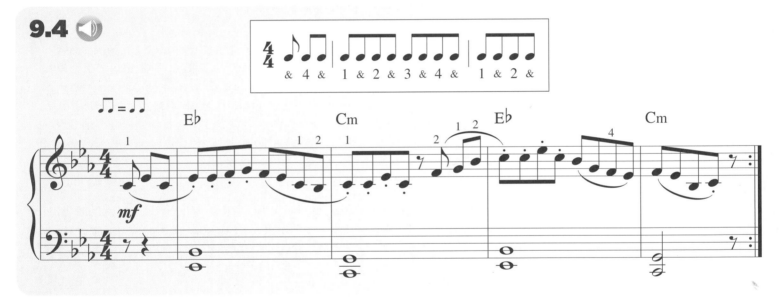

Improvise

Improv No. 31

C Minor Pentatonic Scale

> This improvisation uses the C Minor pentatonic scale (relative of E-flat Major). Listen for the root note C to be used prominently in the Q & A track as a tonal anchor for the melodic phrases.

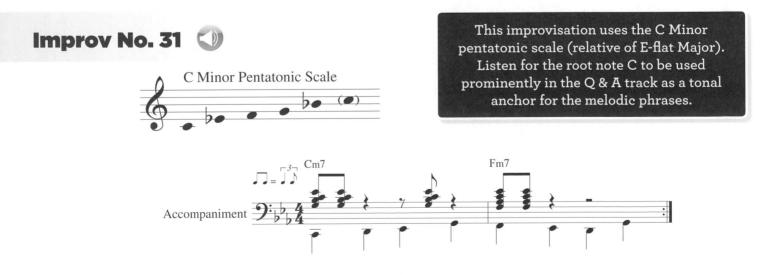

Accompaniment

CHAPTER 10
The Major Blues Scale

The shift from the pentatonic scale to the blues scale is a very small shift indeed. The two scales are, in fact, identical apart from one added pitch:

Simply by inserting this pitch between the 2nd and 3rd scale tones, we transform the major pentatonic scale into the major blues scale! Play the new scale. That added tone is a special one, the ultimate blues note: the lowered (flatted) third. The bright and bluesy sound of the major blues scale makes it extremely popular in all styles. It can be heard in the whistling coda of "(Sittin' On) The Dock of the Bay" by Otis Redding and in the infectious unison instrumental passages of "Sir Duke" by Stevie Wonder. You can also hear its use quite extensively in traditional New Orleans style jazz.

It may be beneficial at this point to clarify a few points about scales and their use. Scales represent sequences of notes that musicians, over time, have found to be useful and versatile. There is no rule book that states when or how a musician must employ a scale. In fact, a musician is free to use any note at any time if it sounds good! However, the most tried-and-true note sequences tend to be those of common scales, and moving too far away from them may sound strange and "outside," depending on the style. This is why it is exceedingly practical to study them. They give us valuable insight to the work and approach of the pros, and provide us a solid foundation from which to build upon.

Ex. 10.1 is a two-octave C Major blues scale, ascending and descending. This will be a great aid in preparation for the exercises and improvisations to follow. You should be in no rush to practice hands together. Rather, take your time working hands separately until the pattern and fingering are secure.

10.1 🔊

You'll be instructed to return to this exercise in preparation for the improvisation sections on page 74 (key of F and G). Audio tracks are available for all three keys.

This page presents the major blues scale phrases first in C, then shifted to F. Sound familiar? It is the same approach we used for the C and F Major pentatonic exercises back on page 62. Take some time to compare the patterns of that page with the patterns on this page. Remember that they will share the same scale tones apart from the added blues note.

10.2

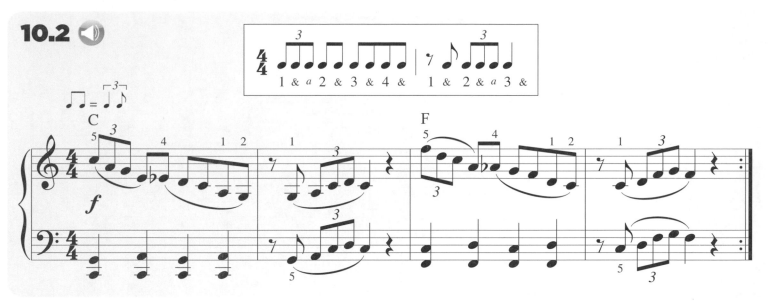

10.3

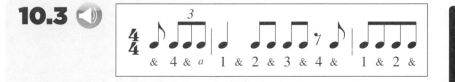

Don't be confused by the presence of both D-sharp and E-flat in the C portion, nor by both G-sharp and A-flat in the F portion. It's customary to use sharps for ascending phrases and flats for descending ones.

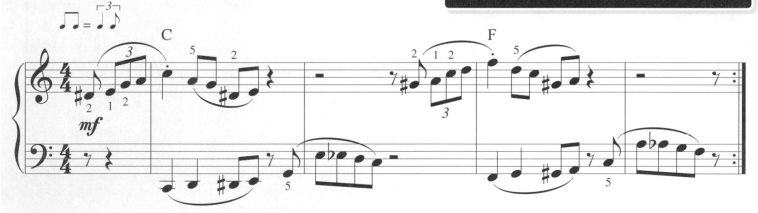

10.4

(non-legato)

You are now ready to explore **Improv No. 32** on page 74.

Compare these D and G Major blues scale patterns to the D and G Major pentatonic patterns found on page 63.

10.5

10.6

10.7

You are now ready to explore **Improv No. 33** on page 74.

Compare these next two exercises to the B-flat and E-flat Major pentatonic exercises on page 64.

10.8 🔊

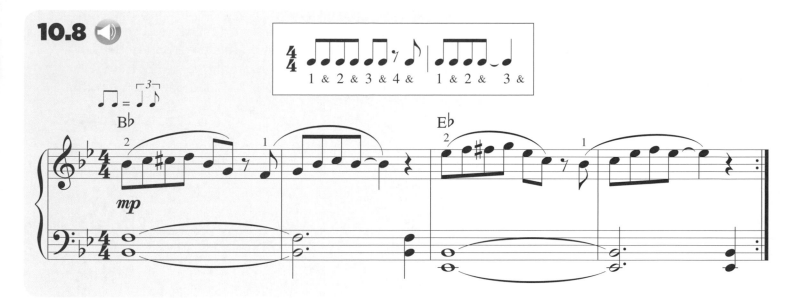

10.9 🔊

10.10 🔊

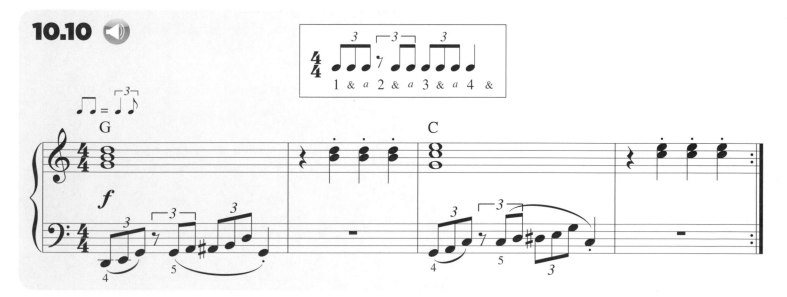

You are now ready to explore **Improv No. 34** on page 74.

Improvise

This improvisation section will feature the major blues scales. As when we first started to use the pentatonic scale, the Q & A track will ease you into things by focusing first on the lower part of the scale (with some neighboring scale tones below), before moving up and incorporating larger portions. The fingering is included as a suggestion, but other combinations can certainly be used depending on the melodic shape of the phrase.

Improv No. 32

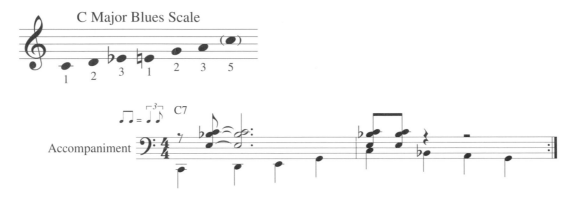

After learning this scale, return to Ex. 10.1 and try that exercise in F! The current fingering will apply since the shapes of the C and F Major blues scales are identical (the blues note is the only black key).

Improv No. 33

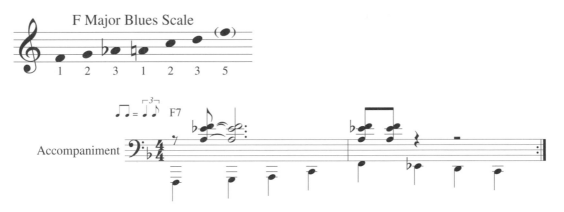

We shift now to the G Major blues scale for our improvisation. In preparation, return once again to Ex. 10.1 and transpose to G. The fingering will be the same.

Improv No. 34

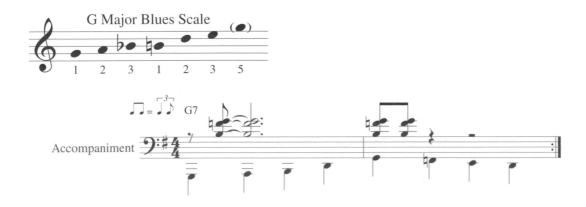

CHAPTER 11
The (Minor) Blues Scale

As you may have guessed, the minor blues scale is the relative minor of the major blues scale. This means, of course, that they share the same pitches; but the tonal center shifts:

Remember that you can quickly determine the relative minor by counting down three half steps from the root of the major. Let's now take a look at how the new scale compares to the minor pentatonic scale:

You may recall that the only difference between the major pentatonic and major blues scales was the addition of one tone to the major blues scale. That tone was the lowered third (the ultimate blues note). But, with the shift to the minor blues scale, the relationship of this tone to the root tone has also shifted. It is now a lowered (flatted) fifth, which is still a very bluesy note!

The minor blues scale is more frequently referred to as just the "blues scale;" hence, the parentheses above. It is helpful to use the term "minor blues" when comparing to, or when playing alongside with, the major blues scale. As the name implies, it is extremely effective when used in minor keys and has been the melodic source for oodles of classic guitar riffs; for example, in Cream's "Sunshine of Your Love," Deep Purple's "Smoke on the Water," and Jethro Tull's "Aqualung." This scale is also surprisingly effective in major keys, as we will soon learn.

The exercises in this chapter will further demonstrate the useful applications of relative major and minor pairings. For example, the three minor blues scales used in the Improvise section are the relative minors to the three major blues scales we used for the previous chapter's improvisations. Such relative pairs not only share the same notes, but often the same application—phrases constructed from one scale may often be applied to the other. It is therefore quite practical to view each relative pair as a unit:

RELATIVE KEYS
C Major – A Minor
F Major – D Minor
G Major – E Minor

Below is a two-octave preparatory minor blues scale exercise. It is presented in A Minor, but, as in the previous section, you'll be asked to return to it and to transpose to two additional keys: D Minor and E Minor. (Audio tracks are available for all three keys.)

11.1

Compare the A Minor and D Minor blues scale phrases on this page to those of the A Minor and D Minor pentatonic scale on page 68, as well as to the C Major and F Major blues scale patterns on page 71.

11.2

11.3

The minor blues scale is also effective when played in a major key. The lowered third and fifth tones in the scale produce an appealing bluesy clash (or "bite") when played against the bright major chord. The chord symbols below represent dominant seventh chords. (We will address these types of chords more fully in Book 2.) The left hand plays the major third and lowered seventh tones of the chords. (Keen observers may have spotted dominant seventh chords used previously, in the right hand of Ex. 8.6!)

11.4

You are now ready to explore **Improv No. 35** on page 79.

The three exercises below contain phrases built from the B Minor blues scale that are then shifted to E Minor. Compare these minor blues scale phrases to those of the B Minor and E Minor pentatonic scales on page 68 and to the D Major and G Major blues scale phrases on page 72.

RELATIVE KEYS
D Major – B Minor
G Major – E Minor

You are now ready to explore **Improv No. 36** on page 79.

Let's move on to phrases using the G Minor and C Minor blues scales. Compare them to those of the G Minor and C Minor pentatonic scales on page 69 and to the B-flat Major and E-flat Major blues scale phrases on page 73.

RELATIVE KEYS
B-flat Major – G Minor
E-flat Major – C Minor

11.8

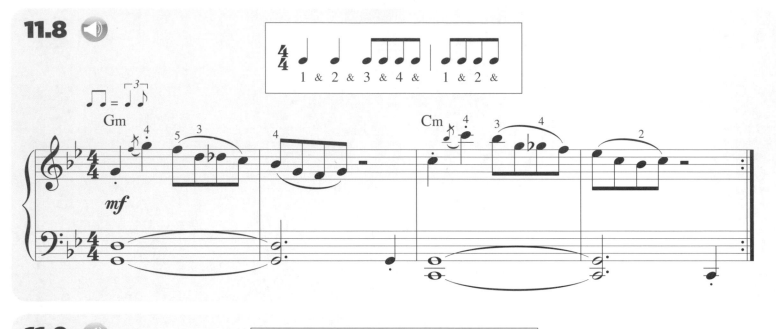

11.9

11.10

You are now ready to explore **Improv No. 37** on page 79.

Improvise

This improvisation will use the A Minor blues scale. Listen for how the "questions" on the Q & A track tend to be centered around the tonic note of A. Of course, when these same notes were used for the C Major blues scale improvisation on page 74, those phrases centered around C. As with Ex. 11.4, we'll use a dominant seventh (rather than minor) accompaniment. For extra credit, try the A Major pentatonic scale when soloing to the Accompaniment play-along track!

Improv No. 35

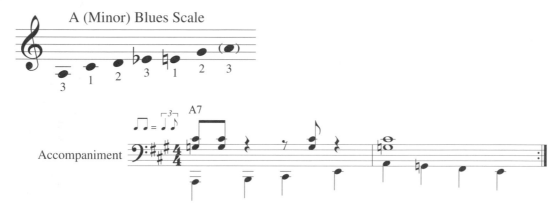

In preparation for this improv, return to Ex. 11.1 (page 75) and transpose to D Minor. Feel free to explore the D Major pentatonic scale (in addition to the D Minor blues scale) when soloing to the Accompaniment track.

Improv No. 36

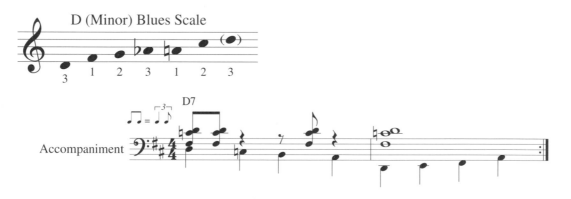

The final improvisation of Book 1 will use the E Minor blues scale. Return to Ex. 11.1 and transpose to E Minor. The bonus scale for the Accompaniment track is the E Major pentatonic.

Improv No. 37

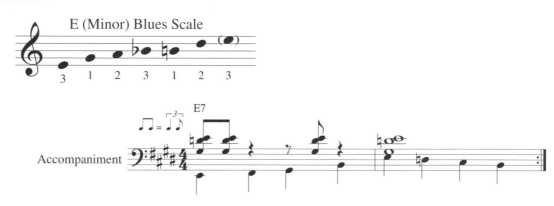

Performance Piece. This entire piece consists of notes only from the D Minor blues scale! Be patient while working out the rhythms of measures 3 through 9. The syncopated rhythms of the right hand coupled with the left hand bass figures will present a challenge, particularly at a fast tempo.

Avenue D

Eric Baumgartner

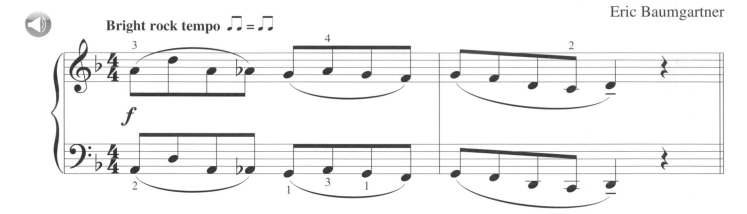

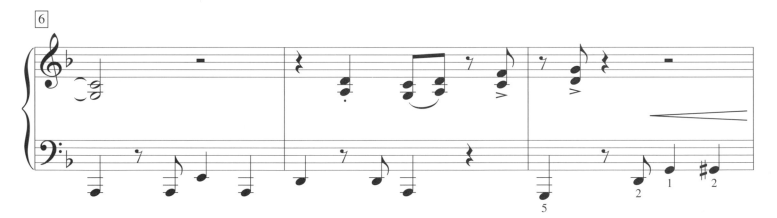

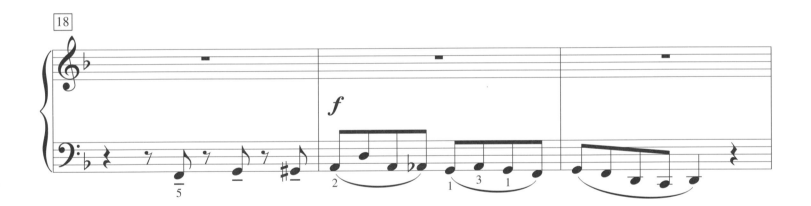

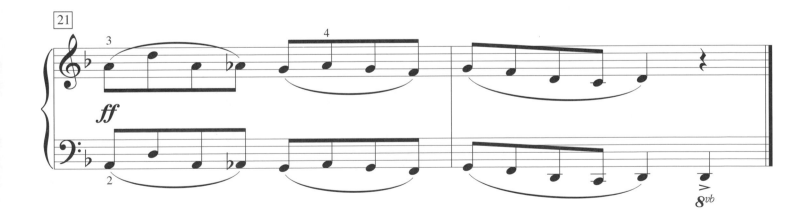

Performance Piece. Here's what I call a rollicking blues number to close out Book 1! The opening right-hand melody (measures 2 through 13) is built from a single scale. Can you name it?

Big Earl's Honky-Tonk Blues

Eric Baumgartner

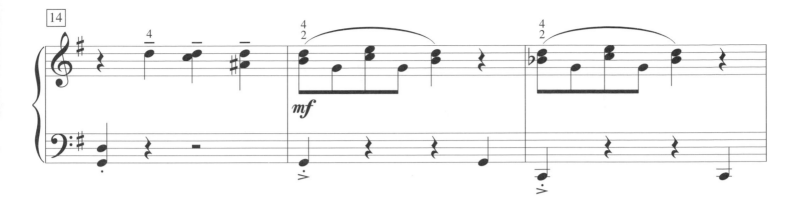

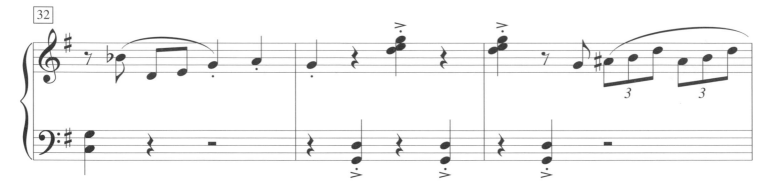

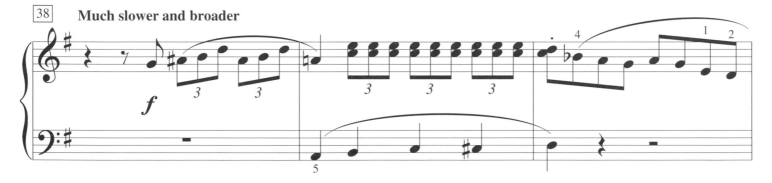

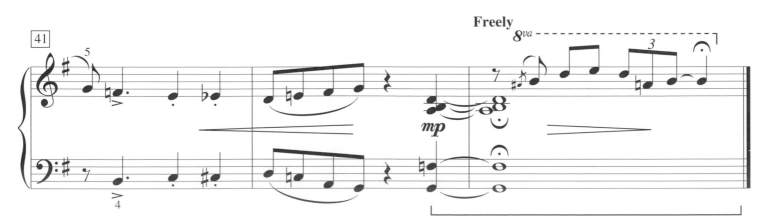

Suggested Listening

Listening to jazz is, of course, a vital part of any jazz student's education. Through careful listening we can absorb stylistic nuances that are simply impossible to capture on the written page. But listening is far more than just an analytical exercise. Once acclimated to its charms, listening to jazz becomes an immensely enjoyable, emotional and rewarding experience.

The list on page 86 may be viewed as a jazz starter's guide, focusing on a narrow period: the mid-50s through the mid-60s. It is by no means meant to be comprehensive. Rather, I chose this period not only for the number of high quality works produced but also for its overall accessibility and popularity. Jazz reached new levels of sophistication during these years while retaining the raw appeal of its bluesy roots. For many (myself included), this period marks the golden age of jazz recordings. Indeed, several of the all-time best-selling jazz albums are on the list.

The selected recordings feature combos rather than large ensembles. These more intimate settings allow the personalities and artistry of the individual musicians to truly shine. The combos are made up with a core trio of bass, drums and piano (or organ or guitar). On many of these recordings, this core is supplemented by one or more brass and woodwind instruments, most typically trumpet and saxophone.

The material is a combination of original compositions and standards (popular songs often taken from Broadway musicals or Hollywood movies). The musicians rely on very simple guidelines when creating the form of their arrangements. The simplicity and uniformity of this framework allows individual musicians to blend in effortlessly with new ensembles, whether on live gigs or in the recording studio.

Here is the layout of a typical jazz form:

INTRODUCTION
Four to eight measures in length.

MELODY
Also referred to as the "head." The most common length is 32 measures (consisting of four 8-measure phrases). The 12-bar blues form is also very popular.

IMPROVISED SOLOS
The musicians typically solo over the same chord sequence as was used for the melody. The whole sequence is called a "chorus" and a player may improvise over many repetitions of the chorus during their solo.

TRADING FOURS
Occasionally before returning to the melody, the members will exchange improvised solos every four measures. This is known as "trading fours." Most commonly, this is a back-and-forth conversation between the melodic instruments and the drums, with the drums taking the last four measures of each 8-measure phrase.

MELODY REVISITED
After the final solo, the head is restated.

CODA
This is a short tag to conclude the piece. Occasionally a fade-out will be used with no hard ending.

There are many variations to this form, but this basic layout will be a useful "road map" allowing you to better follow the form of many jazz pieces.

Here are the selected recordings:

Clifford Brown & Max Roach (1954)
The Modern Jazz Quartet: Django (1956)
Sonny Rollins: Saxophone Colossus (1956)
John Coltrane: Blue Train (1957)
Art Blakey and the Jazz Messengers: Moanin' (1958)
Dave Brubeck: Time Out (1959)
Miles Davis: Kind Of Blue (1959)
Charles Mingus: Mingus Ah Um (1959)
Freddie Hubbard: Open Sesame (1960)
Jimmy Smith: Back at the Chicken Shack (1960)
Wes Montgomery: The Incredible Jazz Guitar of Wes Montgomery (1960)
Bill Evans: Sunday at the Village Vanguard (1961)
Duke Ellington: Money Jungle (1962)
Thelonious Monk: Monk's Dream (1962)
Kenny Burrell: Midnight Blue (1963)
Lee Morgan: The Sidewinder (1963)
Oscar Peterson: Night Train (1963)
Stan Getz and João Gilberto: Getz/Gilberto (1964)
Herbie Hancock: Maiden Voyage (1965)
Horace Silver: Song for My Father (1965)

I encourage you not to limit yourself to this small list! We are so fortunate to have a rich history of recorded jazz, dating all the way back to 1917. It is staggering, the wealth of brilliant performances by so many brilliant artists we now have at our fingertips. Equally staggering is the variety of styles, genres and sub-genres produced over those 100 years as the art form evolved. Ultimately, every student would benefit from familiarizing themselves with the many and varied eras of jazz and the visionary artists who pushed the boundaries. Luckily, with the advent of the internet and music streaming services, such exploration has never been easier. Of course, given the wide variety of music produced, you may not find all the sounds to be to your liking. Be patient! You are bound to find a particular artist or style that resonates with you. I'll close with a small list of artists (not listed above) that represent a number of different jazz eras and genres. Enter the names into a streaming service (such as Spotify or Pandora) to hear samples of their work. If you like what you hear, you'll usually find links for similar artists to explore.

Louis Armstrong	Benny Goodman	Charlie Parker
Count Basie	Herbie Hancock	Bud Powell
Michael Brecker	Hiromi	Tito Puente
Larry Carlton	Billie Holiday	Nina Simone
Nat King Cole	Keith Jarrett	Art Tatum
Ornette Coleman	John McLaughlin	Clark Terry
Chick Corea	Pat Metheny	Fats Waller
Ella Fitzgerald	Brad Mehldau	Weather Report

Eric Baumgartner's *Jazz It Up! Series* are jazz arrangements of well-known tunes that both experienced and beginning jazz pianists will enjoy. The stylized pieces are intentionally written without chord symbols or improvisation sections, although pianists are encouraged to experiment and explore!

  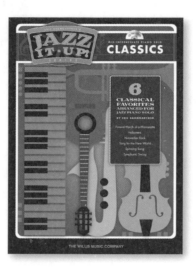 

Christmas
TWELVE CAROLS
Mid-Intermediate Level
Deck the Hall • God Rest Ye Merry, Gentlemen • O Christmas Tree • The Coventry Carol • Good King Wenceslas • Jingle Bells, and more!

00349037 Book/Audio . $12.99

Familiar Favorites
SEVEN FOLK SONGS
Mid-Intermediate Level
All Through the Night • The Erie Canal • Greensleeves • La Cucaracha • Londonderry Air • Scarborough Fair • When the Saints Go Marching In.

00416778 Book/Audio ... $9.95

Classics
SIX CLASSICAL FAVES
Mid-Intermediate Level
Funeral March of a Marionette (Gounod) • Habanera (Bizet) • Nutcracker Rock (Tchaikovsky) • Song for the New World (Dvořák) • Spinning Song (Ellmenreich) • Symphonic Swing (Mozart).

00416867 Book/Audio ... $9.99

Standards
SEVEN FAVORITE CLASSICS
Mid-Intermediate Level
Ain't Misbehavin' • Autumn Leaves • Don't Get Around Much Anymore • God Bless' the Child • One Note Samba • Stormy Weather • Take Five.

00416903 Book/Audio . $14.99

View sample pages and hear audio excerpts online at www.halleonard.com

WILLIS MUSIC

EXCLUSIVELY DISTRIBUTED BY

HAL•LEONARD®